FROM CHALLENGE TO CHAMPION

INSPIRING STORIES OF FOOTBALL GREATS

FROM CHALLENGE TO CHAMPION

12 UPLIFTING TALES FOR KIDS

SKYLER TREPEL

Illustrated by Lorenzo Fornaciari

Z KIDS • NEW YORK

Z Kids
An imprint of Zeitgeist™
A division of Penguin Random House LLC
1745 Broadway, New York, NY 10019
zeitgeistpublishing.com
penguinrandomhouse.com

ISBN: 9798217151387
Ebook ISBN: 9798217151370

Printed in the United States of America
1st Printing

Illustrations by Lorenzo Fornaciari
Book design by Katy Brown
Author photograph © by Kayla Gordon
Illustrator photograph © by Jacopo Mastrangelo
Edited by Ada Fung

To Dad and Zaidy: thank you for many great chats and lessons about football and life. You've always shown that hard work and persistence lead to success.

CONTENTS

HELLO, FOOTBALL FANS!

My name is Skyler, and just like you, I am a big football fan! My love for the game began when my Zaidy (grandfather) showed me videotapes of Dan Marino and the Miami Dolphins. After that, I began regularly watching football with my dad. And like many families, we would all gather and watch the Super Bowl together!

I also played *Madden* and fantasy football with friends and learned about every statistic and player I could. I even played tackle football briefly before switching to flag football. This safer form of the game is gaining popularity among boys and girls and is becoming so popular that it will be included for the first time in the 2028 Olympics!

But my favorite part? The inspirational stories of the players! In this book, you'll read about all-time greats like Jerry Rice, Joe Montana, Peyton Manning, and Tom Brady, as well as some of today's best players, including Lamar Jackson, Patrick Mahomes, Saquon Barkley, and Josh Allen. All the players in this book believed in themselves (even when others didn't), learned from their challenges, and worked hard to achieve their goals.

I hope these stories give you a greater appreciation for the sport, its players, and their life lessons. Use these lessons to follow any dream *you* have as you go from challenge to champion!

FOOTBALL WORDS TO KNOW

Here's a list of football words that will be helpful to know before you read the stories. You can flip back to these pages anytime you don't understand a word.

NFL season: Begins with three weeks of preseason in August, followed by the regular season from September to early January. Then comes the postseason, which consists of the wild card, divisional round, conference championship games, and the Super Bowl in February. For example, the 2024 season began in August 2024 and ended in February 2025.

Quarterback: The quarterback gets the ball on almost every play, passing the ball to a receiver or handing it off to a running back.

Running back: This player gets the ball on running plays. Their yards and touchdowns are often called rushing yards or rushing touchdowns.

Wide receiver: This player starts on the line of scrimmage and is often who the quarterback throws the ball to.

Tight end: This player catches like a wide receiver, but they are bigger, as they must block, too.

Offensive linemen: They protect the quarterback from getting tackled and block defenders to create space for the running back.

Defensive linemen: They try to get around the offensive linemen so they can sack the quarterback or tackle the running back.

Cornerback: This defensive player tries to stop players on offense from catching the ball.

Safety: This last line of defense is at the back of the field to stop long plays or tackle an offensive player who has gotten through everyone else.

Linebackers: They line up between the safeties and cornerbacks and defensive linemen and try to sack the quarterback, tackle the running back, or stop receivers from catching the ball.

Special teams: This includes the field goal, punting, kickoff, kick-return, and punt-return units. The kicker kicks field goals and kicks the ball to the other team after they score and at the start of each half. The punter often kicks the ball to the other team on fourth down when the offense is too close to their own end zone.

Downs/first down: The offense must gain 10 yards for a first down. They have four tries (called downs) to do this, and if they don't, the other team gets the ball.

Snap: When the center offensive lineman hands off the ball to the quarterback by throwing it backward between his legs to begin the play.

Line of scrimmage: The starting point where the center snaps the ball to the quarterback.

Touchdown: When a team scores the ball into the area at the end of the field called the end zone, they get a touchdown (worth six points).

Field goal: A kick through the goalposts (worth three points). Offenses attempt field goals if they feel they are close enough to the back of the end zone and don't want to try for a fourth down.

Extra point: After scoring a touchdown, a team tries to kick a 33-yard field goal for one extra point. Before 2015, the field goal distance was 20 yards.

Two-point conversion: Instead of kicking an extra point, a team can run a two-yard play into the end zone to try to score two points after a touchdown.

Turnover: When the defense takes away the ball from the opponent through a fumble or interception, and their team then goes on offense.

Sack: When the quarterback is tackled behind the line of scrimmage for a loss of yards.

Fumble: When an offensive player loses the ball during play. The team that recovers the ball first is then on offense.

Interception: When the quarterback throws a pass that is caught by the opposing defense. The team that catches the ball is then on offense.

1972 MIAMI DOLPHINS

1

1972 MIAMI DOLPHINS

TEAM STARS

Don Shula
coach

Bob Griese
quarterback

Earl Morrall
quarterback

Larry Csonka
running back

Mercury Morris
running back

Jake Scott
safety

Larry Little
offensive lineman

Jim Langer
offensive lineman

Manny Fernandez
defensive tackle

TEAM ACHIEVEMENTS

- Undefeated season
- Super Bowl 7 champions
- Named the greatest team of all time by the NFL

CLUTCH PLAYS

- Bob Griese faked a pass to Larry Csonka, but threw a touchdown to tight end Jim Mandich to win their third regular season game with less than two minutes left.
- During the AFC Championship, the Pittsburgh Steelers scored in the fourth quarter to make it a four-point game, but the Dolphins' "No-Name Defense" got two interceptions to seal the win.

Perfect. That's the best way to describe the 1972 Miami Dolphins. Led by Don Shula, the coach with the most wins of all time (to this very day!), the 1972 Dolphins are the only team in NFL history to win every regular season game, every playoff game, and the Super Bowl.

The story of the 1972 Dolphins really began in 1970, when Shula became their head coach. He worked his players hard on the field, and helped build team chemistry by holding regular team meetings with them, sometimes late into the night. He wanted the players to be themselves and get to know each other by having fun, too. That season, they won ten games—the season before Shula arrived, they won only three.

In their 1971 season, they made it to the Super Bowl, but lost to the Dallas Cowboys in a blowout. The team came back for the 1972 season motivated and ready to win. Coach Shula told his players that their goal should be to win every game and the Super Bowl.

The Dolphins won their first game of the season against the Kansas City Chiefs by 10 points. But even though they started strong, it wasn't always easy. They almost lost against the Minnesota Vikings. Down 14-6 in the fourth quarter, Coach Shula took a risk. Shula ran a play in which quarterback Bob Griese faked a pass to superstar running back Larry Csonka but instead passed to tight end Jim Mandich, one of the lesser-known players on the team. The Dolphins ended up winning 16-14. They stuck together and won games in different ways, even if their best players weren't the ones used to make big plays.

The Dolphins would face their greatest challenge yet in their fifth game, against the Chargers. Griese went down with a broken leg. Shula turned to 38-year-old backup quarterback Earl Morrall to replace him. Morrall was considered very old for an NFL player at this time. Still, the team supported him, and they worked together.

One way the Dolphins worked together was through a strong running game. Csonka was a big, strong running back. The team had two other good running backs: Jim Kiick and Mercury Morris. Kiick had been playing more than Morris, but Shula believed that Morris's speed made him a better fit with Csonka. Kiick gave up playing time so the running game

would succeed. Together, Csonka and Morris became the first running backs to run for over 1,000 yards each in a season.

The Dolphins offensive line also deserves credit for the running game's success. Their strong blocking created space for Csonka and Morris to run past their opponents' defense. Two of the Dolphins' offensive linemen, Larry Little and Jim Langer, were later inducted into the Pro Football Hall of Fame.

The Dolphins defense was also important to their undefeated run. Super Bowl–winning Dallas Cowboys coach Tom Landry had called them the "No-Name Defense" in a magazine article, meaning that they were a team of players that no one knew. The Dolphins chose not to get upset. Instead, they stuck Landry's quote on the wall of their meeting room and let it motivate them. Their defense may not have had big-name players, but they were very smart and practiced hard. In fact, they became the NFL's number-one defense that year, with players like Nick Buoniconti, Manny Fernandez, Jake Scott, Bill Stanfill, and Dick Anderson.

All these things led the Dolphins to nine straight wins to start the season, and Coach Shula became the youngest coach to ever win 100 games. He said, "You know, the highlight of the year isn't 100 victories. That's not what I'm looking for. [. . .] The thing I want is a team thing, and the height of a team accomplishment is a Super Bowl victory."

The Dolphins were getting national attention. They appeared on magazine covers everywhere, but Shula kept the Dolphins focused on their goal of winning a Super Bowl. Even as his team kept winning, Shula wanted them to keep improving. The Dolphins won their last game of the regular season against Shula's old team, the Colts. With that win, the Dolphins became the first team to ever go undefeated in the regular season!

In the playoffs, the Dolphins kept believing that everyone on the team was important, and anyone could help them win. In their first playoff game, the Dolphins were down to the Cleveland Browns late in the fourth quarter. Kiick, who had given up his role to Morris earlier in the season, stepped up for a late touchdown. Morris and Kiick hugged after his touchdown, showing how close this team was.

DID YOU KNOW?

The Dolphins are the only team from the four major sports (football, baseball, basketball, and hockey) to go undefeated and win the championship.

In the AFC Championship, they had to go up against the Steelers and their star quarterback, Terry Bradshaw, along with their legendary "Steel Curtain" defense. The score was tied at halftime, and the Dolphins weren't playing well. Shula made a big decision. Although Morrall had played great all season, Shula called for Griese to come in as quarterback even though he was just recovering from his injury. This was the spark the Dolphins needed to win the game and make it back to the Super Bowl.

Even after going undefeated, the Dolphins were considered underdogs to Washington in the Super Bowl. People didn't think the Dolphins could win—they remembered their Super Bowl loss the year before. But the Dolphins wouldn't let the doubters get them down. The Dolphins were ready and excited for their chance at a Super Bowl and perfection.

The Dolphins got off to a 14–0 lead, and Csonka ran for over 100 yards. Shula came up with a plan to stop Washington's star running back, Larry Brown. They would stop Brown right at the line of scrimmage, so he couldn't get running. Defensive tackle Manny Fernandez, who had poor eyesight but could make out player's bodies, did this perfectly and made 17 tackles. Safety Jake Scott won the Super Bowl MVP award for making two interceptions. Best of all, the Dolphins won

14-7, completing their perfect season and bringing Shula his first Super Bowl win!

More than 50 years later, the 1972 Dolphins are still the only "perfect" team, and Shula still holds the record for most wins of any coach in NFL history. The 2007 New England Patriots came close, going 18-0, but lost the Super Bowl. The 1972 Dolphins still have a special bond. They've gotten together many times over the years, remembering how they stuck together as a team to achieve historic success, even with all the challenges they faced that season.

JOE MONTANA & JERRY RICE

2

JOE MONTANA & JERRY RICE

MONTANA	RICE
POSITION: Quarterback	**POSITION:** Wide receiver
BIRTH DATE June 11, 1956	**BIRTH DATE** October 13, 1962
HOMETOWN Monongahela, Pennsylvania	**HOMETOWN** Crawford, Mississippi
TEAMS • San Francisco 49ers • Kansas City Chiefs	**TEAMS** • San Francisco 49ers • Oakland Raiders • Seattle Seahawks

CLUTCH PLAY

- During a game in 1987, with two seconds left, Joe threw a pass to Jerry in the corner of the end zone as Jerry leaped in the air to catch the ball and win the game.

TOP ACHIEVEMENTS

- Won two Super Bowls together
- Four combined Super Bowl MVPs
- Pro Football Hall of Fame

Joe Montana and Jerry Rice changed the way football was played, and showed the world what a passing offense could look like. Their success, together and individually, made them one of the greatest quarterback-wide receiver duos in NFL history. But they each had to overcome challenges along the way.

Jerry's challenges began early in his life. He grew up in Crawford, Mississippi—a small Southern town of about 600 people. Jerry's father worked as a brick mason, laying bricks, to support his family of eight children. The money he made wasn't always enough for the family to buy clothes or put a full meal on the table, but they survived. To help his family, young Jerry worked picking crops.

Jerry's life changed when his father took him to work. Laying bricks with his father taught him the value of hard work. It also made Jerry realize that this was not what he wanted to do with his future. At work, Jerry's job was to catch the bricks thrown off the roof.

This was the start of his journey to becoming the greatest receiver of all time. All this time spent catching bricks made catching balls easy for Jerry! Otherwise, there wasn't much to do in such a small town. So, when Jerry wasn't working, he would run for miles. This would also help him in his football career.

Coming from such a small town, Jerry wasn't noticed by many big colleges. But Mississippi Valley State offered him a football scholarship. Jerry knew he had to make the most of his opportunity. He worked harder than other players, staying late after practice to work on his game. For all his hard work, he broke the all-time NCAA receiving touchdowns record and was selected by the San Francisco 49ers in the first round of the draft. He was about to join (and make history with) another legendary player, Joe Montana.

Joe faced a different kind of challenge than Jerry. Joe wasn't as big, strong, or fast as other quarterbacks, and people doubted him.

Joe won a national championship in college, but he wasn't drafted to the NFL until late in the third round, because teams didn't think he was big enough or strong enough to be a good quarterback in the NFL.

But what made Joe special? His ability to keep cool under pressure. When his team was down by a lot, or late in the game, Joe would find a way to play even better and get the win. He earned the nickname "Joe Cool."

Joe's success would later inspire other overlooked quarterbacks like Kurt Warner and Tom Brady. Joe showed that players don't have to let other people's opinions define them. Even though Joe didn't look like a typical quarterback, he had great success through hard work and preparation.

After spending his first year as a backup, Joe became the 49ers starter. In 1981, Joe's third year, he led the 49ers to a 13–3 regular season record, but he wasn't done yet. In the NFC Championship against the Dallas

Cowboys, the 49ers were down by six points with five minutes to go on their own 17-yard line. The Cowboys had been to five Super Bowls and won two while the 49ers were trying to get to their first.

DID YOU KNOW?

In 2010, the NFL Network named Jerry and Joe the best players ever at their positions.

Joe marched his team down the field against the Cowboys. With only 51 seconds left in the game, Joe threw the ball up high in the air to wide receiver Dwight Clark, who leaped up and grabbed the ball in the back of the end zone to win the game and send Joe to his first Super Bowl. This play, known as The Catch, is considered one of the greatest plays in NFL history. The 49ers went on to win the Super Bowl, with Joe winning his first Super Bowl MVP award.

In 1984, Joe led the 49ers to a 15–1 season, and back to the Super Bowl. Up against the Miami Dolphins, led by MVP-winning quarterback Dan Marino, Joe performed when it counted most. He threw for three touchdowns and 331 yards—the most ever in a Super Bowl game at the time, achieving his second Super Bowl win and second Super Bowl MVP award.

Jerry was nervous when he first met Joe in 1985, because Joe had already won two Super Bowls. But Joe made Jerry feel welcome. Joe quickly saw how special Jerry was, and how hard he was willing to work. Receivers were taught to run 10 to 15 yards after making a catch in practice to get used to running after the catch. But Jerry would run 40 to 60 yards, all the way into the end zone, so he could get used to the feeling of scoring touchdowns. Eventually, every receiver started doing this, too. Jerry's leadership impressed Joe.

At times during his rookie year, Jerry struggled to catch the ball. Joe stayed confident in Jerry and told him his hard work would pay off. Joe and Jerry developed a strong bond through their hard work, preparation, and trust in each other. The more they practiced together, the stronger their connection became. It seemed like Joe always knew where Jerry would be on the field.

Jerry admired that Joe didn't always need to throw the long pass. Joe could get the job done by throwing shorter passes and taking his time to get down the field. Jerry was faster than everyone and able to jump higher so he could beat any defensive player covering him. Jerry was also amazing at running long distances after catching a pass, making him a great match for Joe's short passes. Since Jerry could run so fast, this forced Joe to get better at throwing longer passes, too. Together, they both made each other better.

In the 1988 season, they would win their first Super Bowl together. Jerry caught a record-breaking 215 receiving yards and a touchdown during a close back-and-forth game to win Super Bowl MVP. Some of these yards came on a legendary late drive. With just over three minutes left, Joe led his team 92 yards—nearly the entire field—for a game-winning touchdown.

The pair's chemistry continued to grow. The next season, they won another Super

Bowl together, breaking nearly every record as they beat the Denver Broncos 55–10. Joe's five touchdown passes and Jerry's three touchdown catches were both new Super Bowl records. And in the 1990 season, in a game against the Atlanta Falcons, Jerry caught five touchdown passes from Joe—an all-time NFL record. Joe won MVP that year, and Jerry led the league in receptions, receiving yards, and receiving touchdowns.

Jerry said their chemistry was so good, they could communicate on the field just by looking at each other! He explained, "Without chemistry, we couldn't have had the long-term success we did and won so many Super Bowls. But chemistry isn't something that comes naturally. For us, it took countless hours of practice and working together to develop it."

KURT WARNER

3

KURT WARNER

POSITION: Quarterback

BIRTH DATE: June 22, 1971

HOMETOWN: Cedar Rapids, Iowa

COLLEGE: University of Northern Iowa

TEAMS: Iowa Barnstormers (AFL), St. Louis Rams (now the Los Angeles Rams), New York Giants, Arizona Cardinals

BREAKOUT MOMENT

As a 27-year-old undrafted first-year starting quarterback, Kurt led the St. Louis Rams to their first Super Bowl win and was named Super Bowl 34 MVP.

TOP ACHIEVEMENTS

- Two-time NFL MVP
- Super Bowl 34 champion and MVP
- 2008 Walter Payton NFL Man of the Year
- Pro Football Hall of Fame

DID YOU KNOW?

In 2021, Lionsgate released *American Underdog*, a movie about the inspiring story of Kurt Warner's life.

Kurt Warner has one of the most inspirational stories in NFL history. Ever since he watched Joe Montana win a Super Bowl as a little kid, Kurt wanted to be a Super Bowl–winning quarterback. Kurt admired how "Joe Cool" kept calm under pressure and always got up again, no matter how many times he got hit.

Kurt used this inspiration to keep getting up no matter how many times life knocked him down. In college at Northern Iowa, Kurt was never considered good enough to be a starting quarterback or even be the main backup. Kurt's coach told him to start thinking about life after football, but Kurt kept working hard to be ready for his chance.

In 1993, his final year of college, Kurt got his chance to be a starter through his hard work studying the game and proving himself in practice. He showed how ready he was, winning the Gateway Conference Offensive Player of the Year Award. Kurt was excited to enter the NFL draft and prove himself on football's biggest stage.

The only problem? Northern Iowa wasn't a top football school, and players from smaller schools were rarely drafted. Kurt still got an agent and tried to get drafted, but he wasn't picked. In 1994, he was signed by the Green Bay Packers, but they cut him before the regular season started.

Kurt was living with his girlfriend, Brenda, and her two kids, and knew he needed to support his family, even as he pursued his football dreams. He took a job at a Hy-Vee grocery store, stocking shelves for $5.50 an hour. This gave Kurt a stable paycheck, but he felt so far away from his football dreams. Most people

would have given up. But most people aren't Kurt Warner.

Due to his strong arm and accuracy throwing the football, Kurt was recruited by the Iowa Barnstormers, a team in the Arena Football League. Many people didn't think of arena football as "real" football. But Kurt was humble enough to take any opportunity that came his way. He understood that he might have to take a step backward to move forward later.

Arena football wasn't easy for him at first. It's a faster game, and Kurt had to learn to throw very quickly. But he worked hard and adapted to the new game. He led the Barnstormers to the ArenaBowl—the Arena Football League's version of the Super Bowl—and became one of the greatest arena football players of all time.

The St. Louis Rams noticed how well Kurt was playing and signed him to a contract. Kurt spent his first year as a backup, but during the

1999 preseason, the Rams starting quarterback Trent Green got injured. Kurt took over as the Rams starter. His first game would be against the Baltimore Ravens, led by Hall of Fame linebacker Ray Lewis.

Many people doubted that an undrafted 27-year-old first-year starter could be successful. But Kurt didn't let this hold him back. He scored three touchdowns in his first game. Then he did it two more times in a row, becoming the only player to throw three touchdowns in his first three games, until Patrick Mahomes did it in 2018.

Kurt also paved the way for Mahomes with his unique play style. Many of us have seen Mahomes pull off trick plays and wild throws, but Kurt was one of the first quarterbacks to flick the ball from under his chest into a receiver's hands, faking out defenses. All the challenges Kurt learned from, even in arena football, prepared him to succeed.

Kurt won the NFL MVP award in his first year as a starter. More important, he led the Rams to the Super Bowl. By this point, people were paying attention to Kurt's underdog story, and the Rams became known as "The Greatest Show on Turf."

The pressure was on, but Kurt was ready. He threw for a then-Super Bowl record 414 yards, breaking his idol Joe Montana's record. With two minutes left in the game, Kurt threw a 73-yard touchdown on a go-route—when the receiver runs in a straight line down the field—to win the game. Five years after stocking grocery shelves, Kurt was living his dream as a Super Bowl champion and Super Bowl MVP!

Even as an older quarterback, Kurt continued to beat the odds. In the 2001 season, he led the league in touchdown passes and yards and won another MVP award. Kurt and the Rams made it back to the Super Bowl. This time they lost to Tom Brady and the New England Patriots on a last-second field goal in one of the greatest games of all time.

Kurt didn't play as well the following two years, and the Rams released him, less than five years after winning a Super Bowl with him. Kurt played one season with the New

York Giants before signing with the Arizona Cardinals, where he spent most of his time as a backup again. It seemed the league was forgetting about Kurt Warner.

After being counted out yet again, Kurt would prove everyone wrong—again. In 2008, Kurt was announced as the Cardinals starter. That year, he and all-time great wide receiver Larry Fitzgerald became the league's most dynamic duo and were both selected to the Pro Bowl, the NFL's all-star game. In the postseason, Kurt threw for 11 touchdowns, and Larry caught 7 touchdowns—both records for their positions.

At 37 years old, Kurt made it to Super Bowl 43, against the Pittsburgh Steelers. Kurt threw for over 300 yards and three touchdowns. He even threw a 64-yard touchdown up the middle of the field to Larry, who turned a corner and ran it in with 2:37 left to put the Cardinals ahead. Although the Cardinals lost,

Kurt's performance in the 2008 postseason is considered one of the best in NFL history.

Kurt's story is one of the greatest underdog stories in sports history. But Kurt's story isn't great just because he won the Super Bowl. His story is great because of his long, winding road to success and how he had to keep working for it. As Kurt said at his 2017 Pro Football Hall of Fame induction speech, "If you're willing to put yourself and your dreams on the line, at the very least you'll discover an inner strength you may not have known existed."

2001 NEW ENGLAND PATRIOTS

4

2001 NEW ENGLAND PATRIOTS

TEAM STARS

Tom Brady
quarterback

Bill Belichick
coach

Drew Bledsoe
quarterback

Ty Law
cornerback

Adam Vinatieri
kicker

Willie McGinest
linebacker

Tedy Bruschi
linebacker

Antowain Smith
running back

Lawyer Milloy
safety

Troy Brown
wide receiver

TEAM ACHIEVEMENTS

- Won the Patriots' first Super Bowl
- First team to win a Super Bowl after starting the season with a 1-3 record
- Began a dynasty of six Super Bowl wins

CLUTCH PLAYS

- In their first playoff game, Adam Vinatieri kicked two field goals in a heavy snowstorm to tie—and then win—the game.
- Tied 17-17 against the Rams in the fourth quarter of Super Bowl 36, Tom Brady led the Patriots down the field with 1:30 left. Adam Vinatieri then kicked the game-winning field goal.

The New England Patriots of the 2000s and 2010s are perhaps the greatest dynasty in football, and maybe in all of sports. Led by quarterback Tom Brady and coach Bill Belichick, the Patriots won six Super Bowls during this time. This is the most Super Bowls ever won by a quarterback and coach duo, and the most ever for a team. Their dynasty also included an undefeated regular season in 2007. But it all began with their unlikeliest Super Bowl win in the 2001 season.

The Patriots were not thought of as a great team before the 2000s. In the 2000 season, the Patriots went 5-11 with quarterback Drew Bledsoe and first-year head coach Bill Belichick. However, the team believed in Bledsoe so much that they signed him to a 10-year contract worth over $100 million—the largest NFL contract ever at the time. It looked like Bledsoe would be the leader of the team for years to come.

Unfortunately, in their second game of the 2001 season, Bledsoe was hit hard and badly

injured. The whole team was sad and in shock. After all, Bledsoe had been the leader of their team for nearly 10 years. They had to turn to 24-year-old Tom Brady, who was their fourth-string quarterback the year before.

No one thought much of Brady because he was drafted as the 199th pick of the 2000 draft and didn't look very athletic. Even worse, the Patriots had already lost the first two games of the season. Most people wondered how the Patriots would turn their season around with Brady.

Brady wasn't the fastest. He wasn't the biggest. He wasn't the strongest. But he would work the hardest. Brady treated every practice like it was the most important game of his life. The media didn't believe in him, but he earned his teammates' respect with his hard work.

The rest of the team knew they would have to work hard, too. Running backs like Antowain Smith stepped up so Brady didn't always have to pass. The defense, including linebackers Tedy Bruschi and Willie McGinest and cornerback Ty Law, stood strong and stopped opponents from scoring as much. This gave Brady room to make mistakes and learn from them. As safety Lawyer Milloy said, "Sometimes it takes tragedy to bring a community together, a team together. As bad as the Drew Bledsoe situation was, it forced the defense to step up and play as one."

In his first start, with the help of his defense and running backs, Brady and the Patriots beat Peyton Manning and the Indianapolis Colts, 44-13. In their week 5 game against the San Diego Chargers, Brady threw his first game-winning pass for a come-from-behind victory. People started to believe Brady and the Patriots could be something special.

In week 10, Bledsoe was cleared to play. This created a challenge for the Patriots. Who would be the starter? The 100-million-dollar face of the team, or the sixth-round pick who

DID YOU KNOW?

The Patriots dynasty, which began with the 2001 season, is the focus of not one but two TV shows: *Man in the Arena: Tom Brady* and *The Dynasty: New England Patriots*.

was winning games? Most of the team, the media, and even Bledsoe thought Bledsoe would be the starter again. However, Coach Belichick went with Brady. Everyone was shocked. Patriots owner Robert Kraft even tried to change Coach Belichick's mind. But Coach Belichick stuck with who he believed was best for the team—Brady.

In Brady's first game as the starter since that decision, he threw two interceptions in a loss against the St. Louis Rams. People wanted Brady benched and Belichick fired. Bledsoe could have used this to try and force the team to switch quarterbacks. But even though Bledsoe was heartbroken to not be playing, he put his own needs aside to support Brady and help him prepare. This motivated the team to believe in each other even more. This team-first mentality became known as the "Patriot Way," and it would define the Patriots dynasty for the next 20 years.

Belichick chose Brady because he believed Brady had the attitude and leadership of a winner. As Belichick later said, "He prepared extremely hard individually, on his fundamentals, his techniques. Tom, I feel like, got the best out of me because he was so well-prepared that I felt like I had to keep up with his preparation."

Brady and Belichick spent hours watching, studying, and talking about football. On the practice field, Brady worked to learn everything he could, so he improved more quickly than most quarterbacks. Off the field, Brady hung out with his teammates and got to know them, bringing the team closer.

After the early loss to the Rams, the Patriots won every game and made it to the playoffs—their first playoff appearance since

1998. The Patriots were considered underdogs in their first game against the Oakland Raiders. It was snowing heavily, and the Patriots were down 13-3 with eight minutes left in the fourth quarter. To try and throw the Raiders off, the Patriots went with a no-huddle offense, where they would run quick plays without discussing them, trusting what they learned in practice.

Brady led the Patriots down the field with great throws and impressive catches by his receivers. Brady—who had been called "unathletic" by many experts—then ran for a touchdown to make the score 13-10. After the touchdown, the defense got a big stop and Brady once again led the Patriots down the field. The Patriots kicker, Adam Vinatieri, would have to make a 45-yard field goal—in a blizzard—to tie the game. With less than a minute to go and barely able to see the goal posts, Vinatieri did just that! He also made the game-winning field goal in overtime.

The Patriots made the Super Bowl, where they'd face 2000 Super Bowl champions Kurt Warner and the Rams. Almost no one expected the Patriots to win. They knew they would need to play as a team. The Patriots defense was incredibly tough and physical on the Rams' high-powered offense. Pro Bowl cornerback Ty Law ran back an interception for a touchdown to put the Patriots up 7-3 early. Brady threw a touchdown shortly after, and the Patriots were up 14-3 at halftime.

However, the Patriots got a bit too confident. In the fourth quarter, Kurt led the Rams down the field before running in a touchdown. The Rams defense stopped the Patriots from scoring. Then, the Rams offense scored another touchdown to tie the game at 17-17 with 1:30 left.

Bledsoe told Brady that he could still win the game. In one of the most clutch performances in Super Bowl history, Brady got the team into field goal range with a series of well-timed, strong, and accurate throws. Once again, Vinatieri kicked the game-winning field goal, just as the clock hit zero. The legend of Tom Brady, Bill Belichick, and the Patriot Way was officially born.

Brady later reflected on the season that started the Patriots dynasty, saying, "It's like anything. It's progress and it's evolution. It's a series of small steps that seem so insignificant at the time that you're making them that when you look back, you realize the distance traveled."

MICHAEL STRAHAN

5

MICHAEL STRAHAN

POSITION: Defensive end

BIRTH DATE: November 21, 1971

HOMETOWNS: Houston, Texas; Mannheim, West Germany

COLLEGE: Texas Southern University

TEAM: New York Giants

BREAKOUT MOMENT

During his fifth season, Michael recorded 14 sacks, the fourth most in the league.

DID YOU KNOW?

After retiring, Michael became a successful journalist and TV personality, winning two Daytime Emmy Awards and hosting game shows.

TOP ACHIEVEMENTS

- Super Bowl 42 champion
- 2001 NFL Defensive Player of the Year
- NFL 2000s All-Decade Team
- Pro Football Hall of Fame
- Single-season sack record holder

As a kid, Michael Strahan loved watching football with his dad. He dreamed of becoming a professional football player one day. Although he made it, Michael didn't take the usual path to the NFL. Many NFL players start playing football young, but Michael moved around a lot as a kid because his dad was in the military, so he didn't play much football until his last year of high school.

When Michael was nine, his family moved to Germany. Michael didn't know the culture, people, or language, but he learned to love his new home. While Michael enjoyed growing up in Germany, he was bullied for the gap between his two front teeth, which affected the way he spoke. Eventually, he decided this was something that made him special. He said, "You don't want to be like everybody else. You want to be who you're meant to be. And for me, I'm meant to be the guy with the gap tooth smile. Something that used to be the curse—that got me made so much fun of—is now the gift."

Michael played some youth football in Germany but stopped because there wasn't a lot of competition. In Michael's senior year of high school, his dad sent him to Houston, Texas, so he could play football at an American high school. He moved in with his uncle Art, a former defensive lineman in the NFL. Michael was lonely in Texas and struggled to fit in and make new friends.

How did Michael overcome his loneliness? He focused on playing defensive line for his school team and worked toward his dream of playing football in college. He trained with his coaches at school. Michael also spent hours with his uncle in the front yard, working on pass-rushing drills. Michael learned how to run around defenders and use his hands to get around them. He was talented and a quick learner, and he listened to everything his uncle taught him.

Amazingly, Michael earned a scholarship to Texas Southern University after playing just one season of high school football! As a defensive end, he was so powerful that offensive linemen would double-team Michael to try to stop him from getting to the quarterback. Michael's work ethic inspired his teammates. In fact, he was so good that he was named the Division I-AA Defensive Player of the Year his senior year and was drafted by the New York Giants in the second round of the 1993 NFL draft.

Even though he was talented, Michael hadn't played at a top football college or played against other top football players, like a lot of other early round draft picks had. So, it would take Michael a few seasons to adjust to playing in the NFL.

In his first year, he only played in six games because of injuries. But he still worked hard and learned as much as he could from others. Michael learned from his Giants teammate Lawrence Taylor, one of the greatest defensive players ever, to treat practice like it's as important as a game. Michael also followed everything his defensive line coach Earl Leggett taught him, including proper technique and how to learn from watching film of other games and players. Michael believed that if he continued learning, he could be great.

In 1997, Michael finally had his breakout season. He had 14 sacks that year, made the Pro Bowl, and was named First Team All-Pro. The next season, he achieved the same honors while recording 15 sacks. Michael was also becoming the leader of the Giants defense.

His leadership helped the Giants reach Super Bowl 35 at the end of the 2000 season. They didn't win, but Michael came back bigger, stronger, and better to have one of the greatest defensive seasons of all time in 2001. He broke the all-time single-season sack record with 22.5 sacks (a .5 sack means more than one player contributed) and won the NFL Defensive Player of the Year award.

How did he do this? Defensive ends tend to be smaller and run around offensive linemen to get to the quarterback. However, Michael had the perfect combination of strength and speed to run into and through offensive linemen to get to the quarterback. Michael used one move called "the power slip," where he would power an offensive lineman backward and then slip to one side of them to get by for the sack. Michael wasn't just good at tackling quarterbacks; he was quick enough to also tackle running backs. That meant he could disrupt teams' entire offensive game plans.

Over the next few years, Michael continued to be one of the best defensive players. But about 12 years into his career, injuries began to affect his play. It was clear that Michael would retire soon. Still, he came back for one last season in 2007—and his greatest moment yet. The Giants only finished 10-6 in the regular season, but they won all their postseason games to make it to Super Bowl 42 against Tom Brady and the New England Patriots.

The Patriots were undefeated, and everyone expected them to win the Super Bowl. Books had already been written about the Patriots' perfect season. But the Giants used this as motivation. Eventual two-time

Super Bowl MVP Eli Manning was the Giants quarterback, but Michael was the longtime leader who fired up his team with his play on the field—and speeches on the sideline.

On third down in the third quarter, the Patriots were up 7-3. Michael burst through the Patriots offensive line for a game-changing sack on Tom Brady. After the sack, the Patriots tried to earn a first down on their fourth and final down but were unsuccessful. The Giants scored the game's next touchdown, changing the momentum of the game.

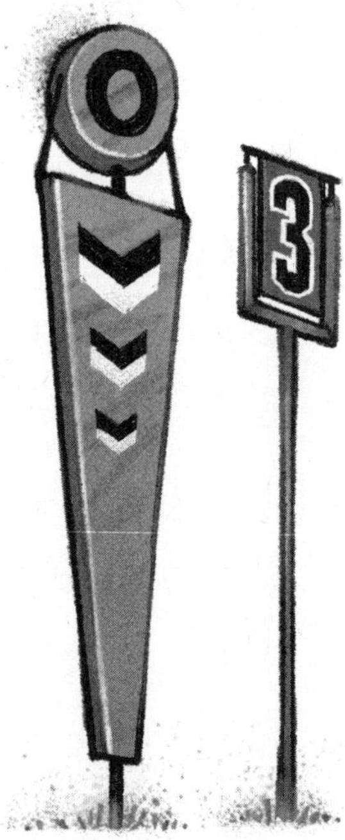

With less than three minutes left and the Giants down 14-10, Michael walked up and down the sideline, pumping up his team. "17-14 is the final [score]. Okay? 17-14, fellas. One touchdown and we're world champions. Believe it and it will happen."

Michael was right. The Giants pulled off one of the

greatest upsets and Super Bowl performances by a defense in NFL history. In a storybook ending, Michael retired after this game as a Super Bowl champion.

With his likable personality and charm, Michael went on to become a successful football broadcaster, television host and journalist, and game show host. Michael later reflected on his journey: "If you believe in what you're trying to accomplish, it'll happen. I mean, anything is possible and I am living proof of that . . . anything is possible as long as you put your mind to it, you believe it, and you enjoy it."

PEYTON MANNING

6

PEYTON MANNING

POSITION: Quarterback

BIRTH DATE: March 24, 1976

HOMETOWN: New Orleans, Louisiana

COLLEGE: University of Tennessee

TEAMS: Indianapolis Colts, Denver Broncos

BREAKOUT MOMENT

In a 2003 prime-time game on *Monday Night Football*, Peyton threw three touchdowns with five minutes left to win the game in a 21-point comeback.

TOP ACHIEVEMENTS

- Two-time Super Bowl champion
- Super Bowl 41 MVP
- Five-time MVP (an NFL record)
- Pro Football Hall of Fame

DID YOU KNOW?

Peyton Manning and his brother Eli have both hosted *Saturday Night Live* and appeared on *The Simpsons*. They co-host the popular alternate *Monday Night Football* broadcast, *Manningcast*.

Peyton Manning is a two-time Super Bowl champion, Super Bowl MVP, and the only five-time MVP in NFL history. This puts him on most people's lists of the greatest quarterbacks of all time. His father, Archie Manning, also played quarterback in the NFL, so many people think Peyton's path was easy. But it was actually full of challenges.

Peyton was born with a cleft palate, a noticeable facial difference where the two parts of the roof of his mouth weren't joined properly, causing a gap in his lip. As a baby, he had to drink out of a special bottle so milk wouldn't come out of his nose. He had two surgeries to close the gap and make sure his mouth could support his teeth. He had to visit the dentist constantly and wear braces because his teeth weren't growing properly.

Peyton was bullied at school because he looked different. The bullying was hard on his mental health, and Peyton bravely asked his family for help. As he later said in a video about mental health, "It's important to talk about it and it's important to go out there and try to get some help. [. . .] Talking about mental health is not a sign of weakness, but really a sign of strength."

Football was a bright light in Peyton's life. He wanted to become the best football player he could be, and he worked hard to achieve his dream. A custodian at Peyton's high school said that while cleaning the schoolyard before five in the morning, he often saw Peyton there, already practicing.

Peyton wasn't very fast or strong, but he worked hard to improve and got his teammates to work out and practice with him. It all paid off—Peyton became a high school football star and was recruited by more than 60 colleges. He won many awards in college, and in 1998, became the number-one draft pick for the Indianapolis Colts.

The Colts weren't very good at the start of Peyton's career, but he grew into a strong leader who helped others improve. When one of the Colts' new receivers, Anthony Gonzalez, had to finish college in Ohio after being drafted, Peyton drove there multiple times a week just to work with him and build a connection.

Peyton stood at a towering height of six feet, five inches and worked hard in the gym. This gave him incredible arm strength for throwing. But he also knew that football was a mental game, so he worked hard to be the most prepared player on the field. He seemed to always know where every player was going to be, and he could change plays at the line of scrimmage just by looking at how the defense was lined up. He also used his smarts to trick defenses into thinking a different play was happening, or to get them to jump early for a penalty. When he wasn't playing or practicing, he was usually watching film of himself or other teams.

Peyton's talent and preparation finally came together to help him lead his team to a 12-4 record in the 2003 season, and earn him his first NFL MVP award. In the AFC Championship, he lost to Tom Brady and the New England Patriots. The next year, Peyton led the league in touchdowns and won MVP again, but he lost to Brady in the playoffs—again.

Brady and Peyton were the top two players in the game, but Brady had already won three Super Bowls, and Peyton hadn't won any. The media talked about Peyton as someone who could only play well in the regular season.

That was about to change. In the 2006 season, Peyton finally beat Brady and the Patriots in the AFC Championship to reach his first Super Bowl, against the Chicago Bears. Before the Super Bowl, he watched every game the Bears played that season to prepare. Peyton won Super Bowl MVP in a 29-17 victory over the Bears. He went on to two more MVP seasons and another Super Bowl appearance with the Colts in the 2009 season.

Unfortunately, in 2011, Peyton suffered a neck injury and needed surgery. Doctors told him he might not be able to return to the NFL. He didn't play for the rest of the season, and the Colts cut him. But Peyton wasn't done playing.

In 2012, the Denver Broncos took a chance on Peyton. He had an excellent season, winning the NFL Comeback Player of the Year award. The following year, Peyton had the best season of his entire career, less than two years after the Colts released him. He won his record fifth MVP award, tied the record for the most touchdowns in a game (7), broke the all-time single-season touchdown record (55), and broke the all-time single-season yards record (5,477). Peyton lost in the Super Bowl that season, but his 16th season in the NFL went down in history as one of the best by a quarterback.

In Peyton's 18th season, his play began to worsen due to all his past injuries. He no longer had the strength to throw big passes. However, just like he knew to ask for help while struggling as a kid, he knew he needed to ask his teammates to help him now. His team stepped up, leading Peyton and the Broncos to a 12–4 record and one final playoff showdown with Brady and the Patriots. The Broncos won to go to Super Bowl 50!

In the Super Bowl, Peyton didn't throw a single touchdown. But he was able to read the Carolina Panthers defense and make the right play calls for his offense. Peyton worked with his running backs and threw short passes to lead his team down the field. The Broncos defense stood strong and shut down MVP Cam Newton and the Panthers. At age 39, Peyton won his second Super Bowl. He retired a month later.

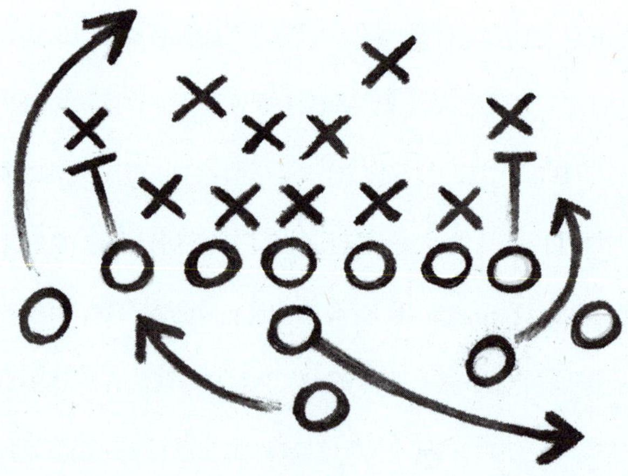

Peyton has used his fame to give back to others. He started the Peyback Foundation to help less fortunate children. He volunteered with his brother Eli (also a two-time Super Bowl champion) after Hurricane Katrina destroyed their hometown of New Orleans to deliver water and other supplies to people in need. He also raised lots of money for a children's hospital in Indiana that is now named after him. The hospital helps all kinds of kids, including many who have facial differences like Peyton had as a kid.

Peyton may be famous and successful, but he reminds people that we're more alike than we think. "So many people look up to NFL players and think just because they're in the NFL and playing at such a high level that they don't have any problems. That's not true," Peyton said. "Everybody has problems. Everybody has things they're dealing with. It's important for them to open up because that will help people realize that it's okay not to be okay."

TROY POLAMALU

7

TROY POLAMALU

POSITION: Safety

BIRTH DATE: April 19, 1981

HOMETOWNS: Santa Ana, California; Tenmile, Oregon

COLLEGE: University of Southern California

TEAM: Pittsburgh Steelers

BREAKOUT MOMENT

During the second game of his third season, Troy tied the NFL record for most sacks by a safety in a game, with three.

TOP ACHIEVEMENTS

- Two-time Super Bowl champion
- 2010 NFL Defensive Player of the Year
- NFL 2000s All-Decade Team
- Pro Football Hall of Fame

DID YOU KNOW?

Troy's black curly hair, which he keeps long as a tribute to his Samoan heritage, was so famous that Head & Shoulders insured his hair for $1 million.

Troy Polamalu is one of the greatest safeties of all time. He won the Super Bowl twice, won NFL Defensive Player of the Year in 2010, and he changed what people thought was possible at the safety position. But he might not have gotten there without making a tough choice: to move away from home as a kid.

When Troy was just a little boy, his father left the family, so his mother had to raise him by herself. They moved to Santa Ana, California, but quickly realized that it wasn't the best place for him to grow up. Troy's older brother, whom he looked up to and played football with, was in and out of jail after getting involved with some bad people.

When he was eight years old, Troy went to visit his aunt and uncle in Tenmile, Oregon. He was only supposed to stay for two weeks, but he ended up staying and going to school there when his mom couldn't leave his siblings to come and get him. At the end of the school year, Troy begged his mom to let him stay in

Oregon. Even though Troy knew he would miss his mom a lot, they both knew he could have a better life there, so she agreed.

Troy's uncle told him that he had to follow the rules and get good grades, or he wouldn't be able to stay. This wasn't easy for Troy at first, but his uncle's strict rules helped shape him into the man and football player he would become. Getting away from the troubles in Santa Ana and living in a stable environment in Oregon helped Troy do well in his classes. Troy was also a naturally talented athlete. He joined his high school football team where he played both offense and defense and won many honors.

While living with his Samoan aunt and uncle, Troy learned more about his background, including the idea of *fa'a Samoa*, or "the Samoan way." To Troy, this meant being a warrior on the field, and a gentleman off it. When he was playing football, Troy was tough and a good tackler. But once the game was over, Troy was humble and polite toward teammates and opponents.

Troy's hard work in high school paid off, and he earned an athletic scholarship to the University of Southern California. He said that God named him Troy (the ancient Turkish city where the Trojan War was fought) because he was born to play for the USC Trojans. By his second season, Troy was named team captain. Legendary head coach Pete Carroll built his defense around the young player.

Troy could do it all. A safety usually stays in the back of the field as the last line of defense, but Troy could make a difference anywhere on the field with his speed, strength, and ability to jump. He could tackle any player, including the quarterback. He made athletic interceptions, diving and catching the ball with one hand. After interceptions, he was strong enough to break tackles and fast enough to run the ball back for a touchdown. Troy was even allowed to break free from the original play call, depending on what opportunities he saw on the field.

Troy was a first-round draft pick for the Pittsburgh Steelers, but his rookie season didn't go as planned. He didn't start a single game that year. Although he had 38 tackles and 2 sacks, they happened at random. He was becoming known as someone who could only be good sometimes. Some journalists said the Steelers shouldn't have picked him. "My rookie season was not enjoyable nor was it very successful," Troy said. "I kind of had a real conversation with myself. I was like, 'Listen man, you're either going to go all-in on this or all-out. Because if you're not all-in on this, there might not be a career.'"

Troy's teammates believed in him, even if the media didn't. Although Troy wasn't ready to start on the field yet, he was ready to learn. Steelers starting safety Mike Logan taught Troy everything he knew about being a safety in the NFL, even though this would make Troy good enough to take his starting job.

Troy did just that in his second season, replacing Mike Logan as the starter. The Steelers defensive coordinator, Dick LeBeau, built the defense around Troy, just like Pete Carroll did at USC. Troy played so well that he earned his first Pro Bowl selection.

In the 2005 season, his second as a starter, Troy was becoming known as one of the NFL's best defensive players. In a game against the Houston Texans, Troy sacked the quarterback three times, tying the single-game sack record for a safety. Troy helped lead the Steelers defense all the way to a Super Bowl win and earned himself another Pro Bowl selection.

By the 2008 season, Troy was changing what the safety position looked like. It seemed like he was everywhere at the same time! And he made the biggest plays when the lights shone the brightest. In the AFC Championship, he caught a pick-six (an interception returned for a touchdown) to send the Steelers to the Super Bowl. After he intercepted the pass, Troy ran across the field to get away from defenders before running straight down the sideline in between a cluster of defenders, carrying the ball above his head for the 40-yard touchdown.

Going up against record-breaking Kurt Warner, Larry Fitzgerald, and the Arizona Cardinals in Super Bowl 43, Troy and the Steelers won their second Super Bowl. Troy's big hair and big plays made him a star. He even made the cover of the *Madden NFL 10* video game, along with Fitzgerald.

In 2010, Troy recorded 63 tackles, 7 interceptions, 11 pass deflections, and a touchdown. He was named the NFL Defensive Player of the Year and led the Steelers to another Super Bowl appearance. The 2011 season was another great one for Troy, but then he began to suffer injuries and concussions that kept him from being able to play as much. In 2015, Troy retired after 12 seasons in the NFL. He knew it was time to take care of his health and spend time with his family.

Troy has given back to his community, spending time with sick kids in the Pittsburgh Children's Hospital, donating to the

Department of Education in American Samoa, and supporting the Neighborhood Resilience Project. He was nominated for the 2010 Walter Payton NFL Man of the Year Award for his community work.

Troy Polamalu helped make the 2000s Steelers defense one of the best of all time. He also proudly represented Samoan culture in football, inspiring fellow Samoan players like Los Angeles Rams wide receiver Puka Nacua, and showing everyone how to take pride in where they come from.

LAURENT DUVERNAY-TARDIF

8

LAURENT DUVERNAY-TARDIF

POSITION: Guard

BIRTH DATE: February 11, 1991

HOMETOWN: Mont-Saint-Hilaire, Quebec

COLLEGE: McGill University

TEAMS: Kansas City Chiefs, New York Jets

BREAKOUT MOMENT

Laurent was named *Sports Illustrated*'s Sportsperson of the Year in 2020 when he took a break from football after winning a Super Bowl to help in a hospital during the pandemic.

TOP ACHIEVEMENTS

- Super Bowl 54 champion
- *Sports Illustrated*'s Sportsperson of the Year
- Northern Star Award
- Named to the Order of Canada

DID YOU KNOW?

Laurent loves sailing and he sailed around the Bahamas for a year with his family when he was 14.

Offensive linemen play an important position in the NFL. They protect the quarterback and create space for the running back by blocking defenders. Even after the play starts, offensive linemen continue to run up the field to block for the ball carriers. Laurent Duvernay-Tardif protected his teammates, but he also worked to protect humanity as one of the only people to play in the NFL while going to medical school to become a doctor.

Growing up, Laurent had many passions. One of those was football, which he loved because of the strategy involved. Another dream he had was to become a doctor. He loved science and wanted to make an impact on people's lives. Laurent didn't want to be limited to just one dream, so he worked hard at both academics and athletics. He was accepted into McGill University, one of the best colleges in Canada, and played football there while attending medical school.

Since the first NFL draft in 1936, only 10 players, including Laurent, have been drafted from a Canadian university, so how did teams notice Laurent? One way was that he was invited to play in the East-West Shrine Bowl, and was coached by some top NFL coaching staff, with NFL scouts watching. Laurent was able to show off his rare combination of size, speed, and strength, which allowed him to stay upright and block with power even as big defenders rushed toward him.

Teams also knew how intelligent he was. You might think that football and becoming a doctor don't have a lot in common, but Laurent knew what he learned from one could help him succeed in the other. As he wrote in the Players' Tribune, "It's difficult not to connect my experiences pursuing medicine to whatever success I've experienced playing football. The discipline required to study medicine—the long hours, the note-taking, the attention to detail—definitely made my transition to the NFL easier. Even just having a better understanding of how to take care of my body with nutrition and hydration has been helpful."

While the 2014 NFL draft was happening, Laurent was working in a hospital as a medical student, helping with a surgery. Since he was working, he had people in the hospital prepared to answer his phone and say yes in case he was drafted! He was drafted—by the Kansas City Chiefs in the sixth round as the

200th pick of the draft. During his first year he sat on the bench, which was okay because it gave him a year to learn the playbook and learn more about playing professionally. He realized how much his note-taking in school was helping him learn the game faster.

Laurent's schedule was intense. During the NFL season, he was in the US, playing football. During the offseason, he was in Canada, attending medical school and working at a hospital. Laurent's passion gave him the energy to work hard at both activities.

In his second season, Laurent earned his spot in the starting lineup as a right guard. His job was to block defensive linemen trying to sack the quarterback from the inside. He got off to an amazing start with the Chiefs, helping them win many games in the regular season, but the team didn't make it far in the playoffs.

He was becoming known as one of the best guards in the NFL, able to block top defenders. However, in 2017, he suffered an MCL sprain, a type of knee injury. Because of his medical experience, he knew what his injury was as soon as it happened, and he knew what he had to do to get back on the field. In May 2018, he graduated from medical school and became the first practicing doctor to play in the NFL.

But in his sixth game of the 2018 season, Laurent fractured a bone in his lower leg. He came back strong for the 2019 season, playing in 14 games. Blocking for Patrick Mahomes, Laurent helped lead the Chiefs all the way to a Super Bowl victory—their first in 50 years!

Laurent had become a champion and hero to football fans, but what he did next was even more heroic. When the COVID-19 pandemic hit in 2020, Laurent decided to put his football career on hold. Even though he'd just become a champion and was in the prime of his career, he went back to Quebec to work in a long-term care facility to care for older people with health problems. His sacrifice during the pandemic inspired many, and he was named

the *Sports Illustrated* Sportsperson of the Year in 2020. He also received the Northern Star Award as Canada's top athlete. In 2024, he was appointed to the Order of Canada for his football career and service to others during the pandemic.

Leaving the NFL was not an easy decision for Laurent. He knew that sports played an important role during the pandemic. People were feeling sad and lonely at home, and sports were a way to help people feel happier and connected. He could have helped his teammates by returning for another Super Bowl run as the defending champions, but Laurent felt he could do the most good helping save lives back in Canada.

Laurent later said, "The decision of opting out of the 2020 season was for sure one of the toughest ones I had to make in my life . . . I [wanted] to play football [the] next year. I just felt like [that] year there were other things more important than football going on and it was really a personal decision. [. . .] What I'm saying is that for me with my background and what I was able to provide, it would have been nonsense not to go back and help." Laurent made a short return to the NFL before announcing his retirement in 2023 to focus on becoming a doctor full-time.

Laurent's incredible story shows that you can have many passions and succeed at them, even if you need to make tough choices between them sometimes. With hard work and belief in yourself, you won't just accomplish one dream—you can accomplish many.

LAMAR JACKSON

9

LAMAR JACKSON

POSITION: Quarterback

BIRTH DATE: January 7, 1997

HOMETOWN: Pompano Beach, Florida

COLLEGE: University of Louisville

TEAM: Baltimore Ravens

BREAKOUT MOMENT

In his first full year as a starter, Lamar led the league in passing touchdowns, set the single-season rushing yards record for a quarterback, and won MVP.

TOP ACHIEVEMENTS

- 2016 Heisman Trophy winner
- Two-time NFL MVP
- All-time rushing yards record for a quarterback
- Four-time AFC North champion

DID YOU KNOW?

Lamar Jackson's mom, Felicia, was his first coach—and is still his manager.

Two-time NFL MVP Lamar Jackson has been beating the odds his whole life. Lamar loved playing football as a little boy and was great at it from a young age. He could already throw the ball 20 yards—60 feet—when he was eight years old!

Life, however, was much more challenging for Lamar than football. When he was eight, Lamar's father and grandmother passed away on the same day. This was very hard for Lamar. His mother, Felicia, was there to help him. She told him that one day things would get better, and he'd make something special of his life. Her positive words helped lift Lamar's spirits. He saw how hard his mom worked to support him and his three younger siblings after his father died. This inspired Lamar to keep working hard at football.

Felicia didn't just work hard to buy her kids food and clothes. She also worked hard to train Lamar so he could become the star football player he dreamed of being. To this day, Lamar still says his mom is the best coach he's ever had. Felicia didn't just encourage Lamar to train hard; she trained hard with him. Every day, they would run laps together. They would run football drills with Lamar's brother, Jamar. Felicia even put on football equipment with them, and sometimes Lamar would even try blocking his mom!

Lamar also studied film of other players—not just quarterbacks, but running backs, too. In games, he didn't just throw the football; he used his quick feet to make fast cuts to change direction and run past defenders. Thanks to his training, Lamar was able to do things people had rarely seen a quarterback do. On his first day of spring practice in high school, he ran 60 yards during a play, which helped him earn the starting quarterback position. Not only did the coach make Lamar the starter, but he also changed the entire offense to make the most of Lamar's running and throwing talent.

Even though his coach saw how Lamar's abilities made him a better quarterback, not everyone agreed. Since Lamar was so fast and athletic, people thought he would be better at other positions. There was a time in the NFL when people mistakenly believed that Black people didn't make good quarterbacks because they weren't smart enough. Most people know this is wrong and racist, but some people still think this way. As a quarterback, Lamar was only ranked as a three-star prospect (out of five possible stars), despite his great talent.

Colleges wanted Lamar to come play for them, but they wanted him to play running back. Lamar would not accept being told he couldn't play quarterback just because he played the position differently than others. The University of Louisville believed in him as a quarterback, so Lamar decided to play there.

Lamar was excited for his first college football game, but it didn't go as planned. Lamar was very worried about throwing an interception on his first play. His nerves made him tense, so that's exactly what happened. But then, just like magic, Lamar's fear of throwing an interception went away.

As Lamar later wrote in the Players' Tribune, "It was kind of a relief to [mess] up right away. It sort of cleared my head. After that, I didn't have to worry about what would happen if I threw an interception. I didn't have to worry about being perfect. All I had to do was go out there and play the game the way I was raised to."

By the next year, Lamar became the best quarterback in college football—and he was only in his second year! He threw for 3,543 yards and 30 touchdowns and ran for 1,571 yards and 21 touchdowns. He won the Heisman Trophy, given to the best player in college football. At the time, he was the youngest player ever to receive the Heisman.

Lamar entered the 2018 NFL draft as a quarterback. He chose not to run the 40-yard dash at the NFL Scouting Combine, an event where top players show off their skills before the draft. Lamar knew he could run faster than most, but he wanted teams to focus on his passing skills.

But even with his amazing play and the Heisman, NFL teams still viewed him as more of a running back than a quarterback. In the NFL draft, five quarterbacks were chosen before him. The Baltimore Ravens drafted Lamar as the final pick in the first round.

In his rookie year, he was the backup to Super Bowl champion quarterback Joe Flacco. But when Flacco got injured, Lamar got his chance to start. Lamar helped lead the Ravens to the AFC North division title. At age 21, he became the youngest quarterback to start an NFL playoff game. Although the Ravens didn't win, Lamar's play earned him the starting spot the next year. The coaches changed the offense to fit Lamar's skills, just like in high school.

In the first game of his first season as a full-time starter, Lamar threw for 324 yards and 5 touchdowns, becoming the youngest player ever to achieve a perfect passer rating (a number that measures how efficient a quarterback is). In the next game, he became the first player ever to pass for 250 yards and run for 120 yards in the same game.

That year, Lamar led the league in touchdown passes and he also broke the all-time single-season rushing record for a quarterback with 1,206 yards. For his achievements, Lamar was named the NFL MVP.

Between 2020 and 2022, Lamar continued to put on amazing performances, including rushing for over 1,000 yards again in the 2020 season, becoming the first quarterback to do so two seasons in a row. Unfortunately, injuries held him and the Ravens back from having the seasons they wanted. In the 2023 season, the Ravens came back strong. Lamar won his second MVP award and led the Ravens to their first AFC Championship game appearance in over 10 years.

During the 2024 season, Lamar became the all-time leader in rushing yards for a quarterback at just 28 years old. He also had his best passing season, with over 4,000 yards and over 40 touchdowns. He became the first player in NFL history to lead the league in both passing yards per attempt and rushing yards per attempt.

Lamar broke another record that year—throwing the fewest interceptions in a season with more than 40 touchdowns. Remember how Lamar's first play in college was throwing an interception? And how he learned to just enjoy the game instead of thinking about what mistakes he might make? I think we can all agree that this lesson worked!

PATRICK MAHOMES & TRAVIS KELCE

10

PATRICK MAHOMES & TRAVIS KELCE

MAHOMES	KELCE
POSITION: Quarterback	**POSITION:** Tight end
BIRTH DATE September 17, 1995	**BIRTH DATE** October 5, 1989
HOMETOWN Tyler, Texas	**HOMETOWN** Cleveland Heights, Ohio
TEAM: Kansas City Chiefs	**TEAM:** Kansas City Chiefs

CLUTCH PLAY

- Patrick threw the game-winning touchdown to Travis in overtime against the Buffalo Bills in the AFC divisional round game of the 2024 season.

TOP ACHIEVEMENTS

- Super Bowls 54, 57, and 58 champions
- Three-time Super Bowl MVP (Mahomes)
- Most playoff touchdowns ever by a receiver-quarterback duo

Travis Kelce and Patrick Mahomes are celebrated as one of the greatest duos in NFL history. Together, they've led the Kansas City Chiefs to three Super Bowl wins as of 2025 and broken many records. Both will end up in the Hall of Fame, with Patrick recognized as one of the best quarterbacks and Travis as one of the best tight ends in history.

Playing in the NFL was a dream come true for Travis, but he almost didn't make it. In college, Travis was spending too much time with friends and wasn't as focused as he needed to be on football. His coach cut him from the team for a year. Travis learned from his mistakes and vowed to work hard and not let his dream slip away. He had an amazing senior year, but NFL teams remembered his history and weren't sure if they wanted to draft him.

Coach Andy Reid and the Kansas City Chiefs took a chance on Travis and selected him in the third round of the draft. But before the season started, Travis suffered a serious knee injury. He only played one snap of football his entire rookie season before getting surgery to fix his knee, ending his season. This was hard for Travis, but he used the time to learn about his body and how not to get injured in the future.

The next season, Travis became the Chiefs' leader in receiving yards, and he kept getting better each year after. No matter who was covering him, he was able to get open to catch a pass. And once he caught the pass, he could gain yards by breaking tackles and running fast. Travis began making Pro Bowls and getting recognized as one of the league's best tight ends.

Unlike Travis, football wasn't Patrick's first love. He loved playing baseball, and his dad played in the MLB (Major League Baseball). Even after he chose to focus on football, Patrick took what he learned from baseball and applied it to football, like throwing sidearm and underhand passes.

Some NFL teams thought of him as more of a baseball player whose different style of play wouldn't work in the NFL. Others thought he would take too much time to develop into a starting quarterback. But Patrick didn't let other people's opinions affect him. He fell to the 10th pick in the 2017 draft, but the Chiefs saw how special he was and took a chance on him.

Patrick was the backup quarterback in his first year, but he worked hard in practice and played well in the final game of the season when he was given the chance to start. The Chiefs made him their starter the next season, and Patrick and Travis's special connection began. Patrick threw for 50 touchdowns in the season—which only Tom

Brady and Peyton Manning had done—and over 5,000 yards. Travis had a then-career high 1,336 yards and 10 touchdowns.

Patrick was only 24 years old. Quarterbacks that young don't usually play as well as he did. And Travis wasn't your typical tight end. Tight ends are usually bigger and slower than wide receivers. And they even block on some plays, so they usually end up with fewer yards and touchdowns than wide receivers. But his combination of size, speed, and strength helped him gain yards and touchdowns like a wide receiver, and he had one of the best seasons ever by a tight end.

Both Patrick and Travis understood how special the other was. As Patrick said, "I remember getting here my first year [and seeing Travis] and I'm like, 'Wait, guys are this big and can run routes like receivers? This is awesome.'" And Travis has said of Patrick, "[He's] the most unique quarterback that we've seen in the NFL, and it's so much fun playing with him because it's almost like we're in the backyard playing."

That 2018 season, they made it to the AFC Championship game but came up against the New England Patriots and another star quarterback–tight end duo: Tom Brady and Rob Gronkowski. Travis caught a key touchdown pass from Patrick in a close game, but the Patriots went on to win.

Knowing how close they were to the Super Bowl, Patrick and Travis came back for the 2019 season even more motivated. That season, they won their first Super Bowl together—and the Chiefs' first in 50 years! But with that success came a lot of pressure on the Chiefs to be the NFL's new dynasty. Brady, Gronkowski, and the Patriots were getting older, and the Chiefs had the best up-and-coming duo in Patrick and Travis.

In the 2020 season, the two continued to dominate. With Patrick throwing the ball, Travis broke the single-season record for

15
KELCE

receiving yards by a tight end. They made it back to the Super Bowl, but lost to Brady and Gronkowski again, who were now with the Tampa Bay Buccaneers.

The 2021 season was another great one for Travis and Patrick, but they lost to the Cincinnati Bengals in the AFC Championship. People were beginning to wonder—would Patrick and Travis win another Super Bowl?

How did they deal with this pressure? With friendship and by doing what they love! Patrick and Travis just focused on playing football and having fun with each other—on and off the field. They play golf together and watch other sports together, and Travis was even a groomsman at Patrick's wedding.

Their friendship off the field is part of what makes their connection so good. As Patrick has said, "A lot of time the routes aren't exactly how we call them, but [Travis] recognizes the coverage, and I know what he's going to do even if we haven't practiced it at all, and I think that comes from us hanging out off the field."

The Chiefs struggled in some games during the 2022 season, but they made it back to the Super Bowl. This was a special—and challenging—one for Travis, because he would be playing against his brother, Jason, who was on the Philadelphia Eagles. Travis wanted to win, but he didn't want his brother to lose.

Patrick also had to overcome his own challenge in that game: a sprained ankle. Doctors said he could play, so Patrick played through the pain. He even ran on his hurt

ankle to lead the Chiefs to a game-winning field goal for their second Super Bowl win. The following season, they won the Super Bowl again in a comeback overtime win. Patrick and Travis had officially turned the Chiefs into the NFL's next dynasty.

The Chiefs made it back to the Super Bowl in the 2024 season, becoming the first team to do so after winning two in a row. Everyone talked about how they could make history with a "three-peat." But they would need to defeat a strong Philadelphia Eagles team, led by quarterback Jalen Hurts and running back Saquon Barkley. In the game, Patrick and Travis struggled. At halftime, the Eagles led 24–0. Patrick had thrown two interceptions while Travis hadn't caught a single pass. The Chiefs ended up losing 40–22, one of their biggest losses ever.

In their seven seasons together, this might be the biggest challenge Patrick and Travis have faced. But Travis and Patrick don't back down from a challenge easily. Travis announced he would come back, at least for another season. And Patrick talked about learning from this loss to get better.

There will be more pressure on them than ever to win another Super Bowl together, but these two love to pull off a huge comeback. No matter what happens, they'll always be one of the best football duos ever, thanks to their bond on and off the field.

DID YOU KNOW?

Patrick and Travis are set to open a restaurant together in Kansas City called 1587 Prime, named after their two numbers.

JOSH ALLEN

11

JOSH ALLEN

POSITION: Quarterback

BIRTH DATE: May 21, 1996

HOMETOWN: Firebaugh, California

COLLEGES: Reedley College and University of Wyoming

TEAM: Buffalo Bills

BREAKOUT MOMENT

In 2020, Josh threw for over 4,500 yards and over 35 touchdowns, leading the Bills to their first division title and AFC Championship appearance in nearly 30 years.

TOP ACHIEVEMENTS

- 2024 NFL MVP
- Five-time AFC East champion
- Most rushing touchdowns by a quarterback in one season in NFL history

DID YOU KNOW?

Josh Allen listens to music from the 1950s and 1960s, including Frank Sinatra, Elvis Presley, Paul Anka, and Sammy Davis Jr. to keep calm before games.

Josh Allen was named the 2024 NFL MVP. But there was a time when no football recruiter considered him valuable at all. Josh grew up on a farm with his parents, his brother, Jason, and two sisters in a small town called Firebaugh, California. Josh and his brother would play video games together and play pranks on their friends and family. Once, they even convinced their friends a gorilla had escaped! His goofy personality is part of what makes Josh such a great and lovable teammate.

Josh and his brother also played multiple sports, including baseball, basketball, swimming, and, of course, football. They had an intense rivalry, which helped sharpen Josh's competitive edge.

In high school, Josh decided he wanted to play quarterback in college. But he played multiple sports and helped at his mother's restaurant and family's farm, so Josh didn't have much time to travel to quarterback camps or work with private coaches. Because of this, no major colleges noticed the small-town farm boy. That wouldn't stop Josh from trying his best near his hometown.

When he was 17, Josh attended a two-day camp at Fresno State, the biggest college near him and his dream school. The school held a tournament where some of the area's best high school players faced off against each other. Josh played well throughout, leading his team to the championship game.

The next day, coaches at the camp were picking the best quarterbacks to practice on the main field where scouts would be watching. Josh wasn't chosen. He was sent to the smaller field, with fewer coaches and scouts watching. The field wasn't even big enough for Josh to show off his arm strength. Did Josh feel sorry for himself? Did Josh quit? No! Sure, he was mad, but he used that moment to motivate himself. He believed that one day he would be the best quarterback from that camp—and sure enough he would be.

His dream school, Fresno State, wasn't interested in Josh. No other major colleges offered him a scholarship or guaranteed playing time. Josh would have to go to a very small college, Reedley College. Josh played his heart out at Reedley and made a highlight tape of his time there. He sent his tape to over 1,000 college coaches, hoping to move to a bigger program so he could get noticed by NFL teams. Guess how many schools emailed him back? Zero!

Josh didn't stop working hard and believing in himself. He focused on improving his strength and speed. He didn't just want to have a strong arm; he wanted to show that he could run fast and break tackles like a running back. Finally, when scouts from the University of Wyoming came to check out football players at Reedley, they recognized how talented Josh was and recruited him to their school, even visiting his farm to meet with his family.

After some great performances at Wyoming, Josh went from receiving zero responses to his emails to becoming a first-round draft pick with the Buffalo Bills in 2018. Josh and the Bills were the perfect match—they were both underdogs. The Bills had become known as one of the worst teams in the NFL. When they drafted Josh, they hadn't won a playoff game in nearly 25 years.

Everyone doubted the Bills for decades, but that was all about to change.

In the 2020 season, Josh led the Bills to their first division title since 1995. He passed for 4,544 yards and 37 touchdowns, which were both team records. He then led the Bills to their first AFC Championship since 1995, where he would go up against the defending Super Bowl champions, Patrick Mahomes and the Kansas City Chiefs. The Bills didn't win, but it set the stage for one of the best games in NFL history the following year.

In the 2021 season, Josh led the Bills to another division title and to the divisional round of the playoffs. The reward? Facing the Chiefs again. They had a back-and-forth high-scoring game, and Josh scored what could have been the game-winning touchdown two times in the final two minutes of the game. The game went to overtime. The Chiefs won the coin toss, chose to get the ball first, and ended up winning 42–36. The game was so close!

At the time, the rule was that if a team scored in overtime, the game ended. Fans, the media, and even other teams really wanted to see what Josh could have done with another chance. After this, the NFL changed the playoff overtime rules so both teams get a chance to have the ball.

Even though Josh lost that game, he earned his reputation as one of the game's best players today. And his rivalry with Patrick Mahomes helped grow the popularity of football's next generation. Josh is no stranger to a good rivalry; after all, he grew up competing with his brother. Now Josh and Patrick's matchups are considered must-watch TV in football, and many people compare their rivalry to that of Tom Brady and Peyton Manning in the 2000s and 2010s.

Josh's arm strength, athleticism, and powerful run game have earned him many records. Not only can Josh throw passes the length of nearly the whole field with perfect aim, but he can also run nearly the whole field while jumping over defenders, too!

Before turning 30, Josh had already broken the record for the most games with two passing and two rushing touchdowns. In 2024, he became the first quarterback to score a passing, rushing, and receiving touchdown in the same game. He also became the first player ever with three passing and three rushing touchdowns in the same game.

All of this earned Josh his first MVP award. One of the people who presented him with the award was Kurt Warner, another famous underdog quarterback. In his speech, Josh could have talked about all the people who doubted him or the 1,000 emails he sent to no responses.

Instead, Josh chose to thank the people who supported him and helped him succeed. "I know this is an individual award and it says 'Most Valuable Player' on it, but I think it's derived from team success, and I love my team. [. . .] We've got such a great locker room in Buffalo, and it takes everybody, from the equipment staff to the training room to the strength staff to Slick Rick in the mailroom to the cafeteria upstairs," Josh said.

Josh is already one of the greatest quarterbacks of his generation. No matter who believed in Josh Allen or didn't, he always believed in himself. This is how he made his dreams come true, and it's something we can all learn from.

JALEN HURTS & SAQUON BARKLEY

12

JALEN HURTS & SAQUON BARKLEY

HURTS	BARKLEY
POSITION: Quarterback	**POSITION:** Running back
BIRTH DATE August 7, 1998	**BIRTH DATE** February 9, 1997
HOMETOWN Houston, Texas	**HOMETOWN** Coplay, Pennsylvania
TEAM: Philadelphia Eagles	**TEAMS:** Philadelphia Eagles, New York Giants

TOP ACHIEVEMENTS

- Super Bowl 59 champions
- First quarterback-running back duo to rush for 13 touchdowns each in one season
- Super Bowl 59 MVP (Hurts)
- 2024 NFL Offensive Player of the Year (Barkley)

CLUTCH PLAY

- In the 2025 NFC divisional round game, Jalen Hurts read the defense and switched the play, handing the ball to Saquon for a 78-yard touchdown to secure the win.

In 2024, Jalen Hurts and Saquon Barkley became teammates—and one of the NFL's most dynamic duos. They even won the Super Bowl in their first season together! However, they had to overcome different challenges to get there.

Coming out of high school, Saquon wasn't even ranked in the top 100 players. He took the first scholarship offered to him, from Rutgers University, but was later recruited by Pennsylvania State University.

Saquon knew Penn State would be a better program for him to develop into the best running back he could be. Although he disappointed some people by not going to Rutgers, Saquon did what would help him achieve his dreams and accepted the new offer.

In college, Saquon became a master at breaking tackles, jumping over defenders, and making quick cuts to get around defenders. Everyone knew how special Saquon was, but he still wanted to do more. As Saquon told *The Athletic*, "I watched film of myself.

I did a self-evaluation. I wanted to get better at finishing the run. Break loose and make another guy miss to get into the end zone." He also focused on catching the ball and other skills like blocking for the quarterback and not turning the ball over.

All of this helped Saquon coming into the NFL. In 2018, Saquon won NFL Offensive Rookie of the Year and made the Pro Bowl with the New York Giants. In 2020, however, Saquon tore his ACL, a knee injury that takes a long time to heal.

Saquon deleted all pictures from his social media, except for one of legendary five-time NBA champion Kobe Bryant. Saquon used Kobe's famous "Mamba Mentality," which is about trying to be better every single day, to inspire him in his recovery.

Saquon came back better than ever. But in 2024, when Saquon was due for a new contract, the Giants didn't want to pay him what he thought he was worth. The

Philadelphia Eagles offered him the contract he was hoping for. Once again, Saquon knew he would be disappointing some people, but he believed he could be the NFL's best running back and wanted to go to a team that believed in him, too. He joined the Eagles, where he would team up with star quarterback Jalen Hurts.

Jalen had his own challenges to overcome—one of which was quite public. Jalen played college football for the University of Alabama, under legendary head coach Nick Saban. Jalen's first season with Alabama was historic.

Jalen broke many records, including the school's single-season record for rushing yards by a quarterback and overall touchdowns, with a combined 36 passing and rushing touchdowns. He even led his team to the College Football National Championship before losing to Clemson. Losing the big game was hard, but it was nothing compared to what happened the next year.

Jalen led Alabama to an 11-1 record and back to the championship game. But with the team down 13-0 at halftime, Coach Saban benched Jalen, replacing him with Tua Tagovailoa, the backup quarterback who went on to play for the Miami Dolphins. This was shocking, because quarterbacks are almost never benched in championship games.

Tua led a comeback and won the game. Tua became the starter the next year, and Jalen was made the backup. Jalen transferred to the University of Oklahoma to get playing time. But his public benching wasn't forgotten. Jalen went from being one of the best college quarterbacks to one of the last picks in the second round of the 2020 draft.

Jalen reflected on his challenges while celebrating his Super Bowl victory in Disney World years later: "Everything happens right on time. [. . .] It's been a journey of highs and lows and different moments where I've had opportunities to learn from. I never ran from any challenges. I didn't let a bump in the road [stop] me from what I envisioned for myself and that's just to be the best man, the best leader, and best player that I can be."

During the draft, journalists asked Jalen the same question they asked Lamar Jackson, because he was Black: Would he play a different position, instead of quarterback? Jalen proved them wrong with a breakout 2022 season. He led the Eagles to 14 wins and a Super Bowl appearance. Jalen broke the record for the most rushing yards and rushing touchdowns by a quarterback in a Super Bowl, but the Eagles still lost to Patrick Mahomes and the Kansas City Chiefs.

The next season, Jalen broke the all-time single-season rushing touchdowns record for a quarterback, but the Eagles lost in the first round of the playoffs. The team knew they would need more help to get back to the Super Bowl. Luckily, one of the best running backs in the game was available: Saquon Barkley.

Jalen and Saquon became one of the most exciting duos in the NFL. Part of what made them so special is that both were double threats. Jalen could play like a quarterback and running back, while Saquon could play like a running back and a wide receiver. In their first game together, Saquon ran for two touchdowns and over 100 yards, and Jalen threw for nearly 300 yards and two touchdowns, including a touchdown pass to Saquon.

In 2024, Saquon had one of the best seasons ever by a running back. He led the league in rushing yards, becoming the ninth player ever to run for over 2,000 yards. This included multiple spectacular touchdown runs of over 60 or 70 yards.

On one incredible play, Jalen threw a pass to Saquon, who gained yards by spinning around a defender and doing another half-spin to get around a second defender before leaping over a third defender—while facing backward!

Although the Eagles kept winning, some people in the media doubted Jalen. He wasn't throwing as many deep passes or touchdowns because Saquon was so good at scoring long touchdowns on the ground.

Some even wondered if Jalen was holding the Eagles back from success. But the Eagles didn't care who was scoring the touchdowns or making the big plays—they just focused on winning as a team. In the NFC Championship, Jalen, Saquon, and the Eagles proved their

doubters wrong with a big win, where Jalen and Saquon each scored three rushing touchdowns.

In the Super Bowl, the Eagles were up against Patrick and the Chiefs again. Could they win this time? The Chiefs were back-to-back Super Bowl champions, but the Eagles had their new, not-so-secret weapon, Saquon. Many believed that if the Eagles won, it would be because of Saquon.

The Chiefs were focused on Saquon, and they were successful in stopping Saquon's running game. But that just opened up what the Eagles offense could do. Because the Chiefs defense focused on Saquon, Jalen was able to throw for 221 yards—40 of those to Saquon—and two

DID YOU KNOW?

After the Super Bowl, Saquon and Jalen were invited on *The Tonight Show Starring Jimmy Fallon*. Saquon said he would only go if their offensive linemen were invited, too, showing his team-first mindset.

touchdowns. With Saquon helping block for him, Jalen ran for 72 yards, breaking his own Super Bowl rushing record for a quarterback. The Eagles won the Super Bowl!

Jalen was named Super Bowl MVP, and Saquon won the NFL Offensive Player of the Year award. In his acceptance speech, Saquon quoted Eagles coach Nick Sirianni: "You can't be great without the greatness of others." Jalen, Saquon, and the Eagles had talked all season about winning as a team—and that's just what they did.

Post-Game Notes

Now that you've read all 12 stories, you know how successful these incredible football players are, and the challenges they've overcome to get there. What can we learn from them?

The 1972 Miami Dolphins and 2001 New England Patriots show that you can achieve greatness together when everyone is a team player and helps each other. Josh Allen and Kurt Warner are two of the greatest football underdog stories. They, and Jalen Hurts and Saquon Barkley, show us the power of believing in yourself, even when others may not. Players like Michael Strahan and Troy Polamalu show that you can finish strong and achieve your dreams, even if you have a tough start.

The stories of Peyton Manning, Joe Montana, and Jerry Rice prove that it's not just about being talented—it takes hard work, too.

Lamar Jackson and Laurent Duvernay-Tardif show that you can be good at many things and don't have to choose just one dream.

And Patrick Mahomes and Travis Kelce show us that success isn't a straight line. Even if you reach your dreams, you may still experience challenges, but you can learn from them and continue to work hard to overcome them.

Now that you've read these stories, think about ways that they inspire you. Ask yourself:

- Which of these stories affected me the most and why?
- What am *I* most passionate about?
- What's a small step I can take to make my dreams a reality?
- What's a challenge I overcame? What did I learn about myself from that experience?

No matter what your dreams are, these stories and questions provide lessons that can help you go from challenge to champion.

12 More Football Stars to Know

There are so many awesome football players! Here are 12 more inspiring athletes you can follow for years to come.

A. J. BROWN (WIDE RECEIVER)

A. J. Brown is one of the NFL's best receivers. He helped lead the Philadelphia Eagles to a Super Bowl 57 appearance, made 3 Pro Bowls, and won Super Bowl 59. You might think a successful football player and Super Bowl champion would always be happy, but A.J. has bravely shared that that's not the case.

In 2021, A.J. opened up about feeling sad and worried often. He reached out for help and has publicly encouraged others to do the same, saying: "It's okay to talk to someone. I didn't think it was okay." A.J.'s words teach us that it's important to talk about feelings and not keep it all inside.

JAYDEN DANIELS (QUARTERBACK)

Washington Commanders quarterback Jayden Daniels is one of the brightest young NFL players. However, going into high school, Jayden was so small that he needed to get a doctor's note to play football. He didn't let that stop him. Jayden scored 50 total touchdowns during his 2023 college football season and won the Heisman Trophy.

In 2024, Jayden broke the record for most rushing yards by a rookie quarterback, won Offensive Rookie of the Year, and played in the NFC Championship—and he's just getting started!

AHMAD "SAUCE" GARDNER (CORNERBACK)

New York Jets cornerback Sauce Gardner got his nickname from his youth football coach. One day, after Ahmad made a great play, his coach called him "A1 Sauce Sweet Feet Gardner." Ahmad liked the nickname so much, he shortened it to "Sauce" and kept it! Now everyone knows his name because he's one of the best cornerbacks in the NFL.

Sauce began playing flag football when he was four years old. Even at that young age, he was determined to play in the NFL. He worked so hard and became so athletic that he played both wide receiver and cornerback in high school, then cornerback in college.

In 2022, Sauce was the first rookie cornerback to be named First Team All-Pro in over 40 years and won the NFL Defensive Rookie of the Year award. In 2023, he became the first cornerback ever to be named First Team All-Pro in his first two seasons.

DAMAR HAMLIN (SAFETY)

Damar Hamlin was drafted by the Buffalo Bills in 2021 and worked hard to become their starting safety in 2022. But in 2023, during a game against the Cincinnati Bengals, Damar went into cardiac arrest when his heart stopped beating after a hit. Doctors rushed onto the field and got his heart beating again, and Damar was immediately taken to a hospital. Within two weeks, Damar was back on the field cheering on his teammates even though he couldn't play.

He won the George Halas Award that year for overcoming challenges, and presented the Pat Tillman Award for Service to the Bills training staff for saving his life. In 2024, Damar returned to football, coming back better than ever with a new appreciation for life and the game.

JOSH JACOBS (RUNNING BACK)

Green Bay Packers running back Josh Jacobs overcame big challenges as a child. Josh's family didn't have much money and experienced homelessness. But Josh never gave up on himself and his football dreams. He broke records in high school and won a championship with the University of Alabama.

Josh is now one of the best running backs in the league. Drafted in 2019, Josh ran for over 1,000 yards in his first two seasons, making the Pro Bowl in 2020. He led the league in rushing yards in 2022 and made the Pro Bowl again in 2022 and 2024.

In a 2020 Super Bowl commercial, Josh gave advice to his younger self: "It's going to be hard growing up homeless, but you've got to believe in yourself. Be tougher than the world around you. And that field? That's your proving ground."

JUSTIN JEFFERSON (WIDE RECEIVER)

Justin Jefferson has made a name for himself as one of the best and most fun wide receivers in the NFL. But he started as a low three-star prospect in high school who didn't record a catch in his first year of college. With hard work and belief in himself, Justin became one of the best college receivers, helping Louisiana State University win the 2020 national championship.

Drafted by the Minnesota Vikings, he became the first rookie receiver in over 60 years to top 1,400 yards and was named to the Pro Bowl. In 2022, he recorded 1,809 yards, becoming the youngest receiver to lead the league in yards.

Along with amazing one-hand catches, Justin is known for his fun touchdown celebrations, like the "griddy" dance, shown in the video game *Fortnite*. Justin was also part of the Netflix show *Receiver*.

YOUNGHOE KOO (KICKER)

Most NFL players are American. Younghoe Koo was born in Seoul, South Korea, which makes his story even more amazing. He has become one of the league's top kickers.

Younghoe moved to the United States, barely able to speak English, but sports helped him make friends and learn the new language. He played soccer before making his high school football team as their kicker. Although he made 19 out of 20 field goals in his final college season, he went undrafted. The Los Angeles Chargers signed him, but cut him a few months later.

Younghoe didn't give up on his dream. He took a year off from football before joining the Alliance of American Football, a smaller league. Younghoe made it back to the NFL with the Atlanta Falcons in 2019. He led the league in scoring and became the first South Korean special teams player to make the Pro Bowl. Since then, he has kicked many game-winning field goals on NFL fields across the country.

PUKA NACUA (WIDE RECEIVER)

Puka Nacua, one of the NFL's best wide receivers, loved football as a little boy. He shared that passion with his dad, and they would watch film and train together. Puka is Samoan, and he admired and studied fellow Samoan Troy Polamalu. By studying Troy's skills, Puka became a unique player with the speed and ball-catching skills of a wide receiver and the strength of a safety.

Puka's dad passed away when he was 11, so Puka's mom had to raise the family as a single mother. Puka, inspired by his father's training and his mother's strength, worked hard to become the best football player he could be.

In 2023, Puka was drafted by the Los Angeles Rams and broke the record for most receiving yards and receptions by a rookie. He is set up for a long, successful career to come.

BROCK PURDY (QUARTERBACK)

Brock Purdy began his career with the nickname "Mr. Irrelevant" because he was picked last in the 2022 draft, by the San Francisco 49ers. He started his career as the third-string quarterback, but when the two quarterbacks ahead of him got injured, Brock stepped up. He won all five of his starts in his rookie year—including a big win against Tom Brady and the Buccaneers—and led the 49ers to the NFC Championship game.

In the 2023 season, Brock led the 49ers all the way to a Super Bowl appearance against Patrick Mahomes and the Chiefs—all before turning 25. His nickname now? Mr. Relevant.

AMON-RA ST. BROWN (WIDE RECEIVER)

Featured in Netflix's show *Receiver*, Amon-Ra St. Brown is one of the best receivers of the 2020s. Amon-Ra started playing sports when he was four years old. His dad, a professional weightlifter and bodybuilder, told Amon-Ra that if he worked and trained hard, he could make it to the NFL. Even though his father expected a lot out of him, Amon-Ra believed in working hard and followed his advice. He weight-trained when he was old enough and caught 202 balls after practice each day—because he'd heard someone else was catching 200.

Amon-Ra was drafted in the fourth round by the Detroit Lions, which was lower than expected. So, he worked hard to become one of the league's best receivers, making the Pro Bowl three times.

In the 2023 season, he helped lead the Lions to their first playoff win in over 30 years and to the NFC Championship game. But Amon-Ra's not done—he has many more dreams to achieve.

C. J. STROUD (QUARTERBACK)

C. J. Stroud's childhood changed when he was 13. His father went to jail, and his mother had to raise him and his three siblings on her own. The family didn't have much money. But C.J. didn't let that stop him from becoming a talented quarterback who could throw far and run fast.

As a teen, C.J. didn't want his mom to have to spend more money, so he would play games with cleats that were too small for him without telling anyone. When people found out about this, they helped C.J. and his mom buy basic supplies.

C.J. went on to become one of the best players in college and was drafted by the Houston Texans. He became the youngest quarterback to ever win a playoff game and turned the Texans from one of the league's worst teams to a regular playoff team with his skills and clutch plays. C.J. also created his own charity to help single mothers.

PATRICK SURTAIN II (CORNERBACK)

Patrick Surtain II won the 2024 NFL Defensive Player of the Year award at only 24 years old. Cornerbacks don't usually win this award, and it can be hard for cornerbacks to show how good they are. If cornerbacks are good, quarterbacks often don't throw their way and risk getting intercepted. And if quarterbacks aren't throwing their way, cornerbacks can't prove that they can make a big play.

So how did Patrick do it? He still made big plays, including 4 interceptions, 11 passes defended, a forced fumble, and a fumble recovery. On one of the interceptions, he ran it back 100 yards for a touchdown. Patrick's numbers also show how little quarterbacks threw his way. He was only targeted on 10.9 percent of snaps, the lowest in the league for cornerbacks. All of Patrick's efforts helped him secure this award.

Acknowledgments

Just like every football team only works through teamwork and a group of people coming together, this book would not be possible without many people helping me along the way.

Thank you so much to my mom and dad for always supporting me and believing in me and my dreams. Mom, your unique career path and love for me has been hugely inspirational. Dad, I have loved our lifelong bond of watching football together and the fact that you're the first person I call when an exciting trade happens or a big game is on. Those Brady comebacks we watched wouldn't have been so inspiring if I hadn't been inspired by your own work ethic. Thank you to my Nonna for loving sports so much, being such an avid reader, and showing me how exciting football can be, by yelling happily at the TV about the Winnipeg Blue Bombers CFL team! Nonna, you and your positive attitude still inspire me every day. Thank you to my Grams and Zaidy for showing me those Dan Marino tapes all those years ago, and to my Zaidy for his love of the Miami Dolphins. Zaidy, your work ethic was incredible, just like the players you admire, and I will always remember your five D's: drive, desire, dedication, determination, and do it!

Thank you so much to the incredible team I've gotten to work with at Penguin Random House and Zeitgeist Publishing, including my phenomenally talented editor, Ada Fung; my expert marketing professional, Portia Turner; Tahra Seplowin in acquisitions for recognizing my passion; my collaborative development editor, Patty Consolazio; my detail-oriented copy editor, Ariel Keith; my meticulous proofreader, Dan Janeck; my capable and thorough production editor, Erica Ferguson; and the brilliantly creative Katy Brown and Lorenzo Fornaciari. Thank you so much to everyone else who made this book possible!

About the Author

Skyler Trepel is a multimedia sports and entertainment journalist and author from Winnipeg, Manitoba, Canada. Skyler has his bachelor of commerce with honors from the University of Manitoba, his film production diploma from the Toronto Film School, and his master of arts in specialized journalism from the University of Southern California.

Formerly a financial advisor, Skyler left that career to pursue his passion for sports and entertainment journalism and writing. He has written hundreds of articles for various publications and is currently a contributing sports and entertainment writer for *People* magazine/People.com and *Entertainment Weekly*. When not writing, Skyler loves spending time with his family, watching and playing sports, cooking, going to concerts, traveling, reading, spending time with friends, playing video games, watching TV and movies, and hanging out with his cat, Simba.

About the Illustrator

Lorenzo Fornaciari is an illustrator, graphic designer, and teacher. He has loved drawing his whole life, and after attending Scuola Internazionale di Comics in Reggio Emilia, Italy, he began work as a freelance illustrator. He has lived in the UK and Italy while creating illustrations for children's books, and was a teacher of storyboarding and Photoshop at Scuola Internazionale di Comics. He has worked on many exciting projects, from video games and animation to websites, comics, and board games.

SCORE THE REST OF THE BOOKS IN THE

FROM CHALLENGE TO CHAMPION

SERIES!

"From overcoming challenges to advocating for change, *From Challenge to Champion* shows how true champions inspire us both on and off the field."

—ALLYSON FELIX, seven-time Olympic gold medalist and founder of Saysh

Stories of top athletes like Simone Biles, Serena Williams, Lionel Messi, LeBron James, and others highlight the power of hard work and perseverance.

Featuring NFL stars like Saquon Barkley, Josh Allen, and Jerry Rice, read about the challenges these athletes have overcome on their path to triumph.

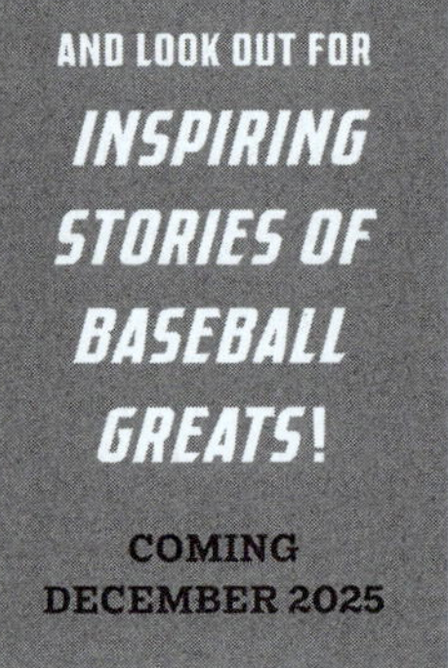

Aaron Judge. Shohei Ohtani. Reggie Jackson. What do they share? Resilience and the drive to win! Read about top MLB players in this fact-packed book.

Parents and caregivers can learn more about these books and upcoming titles at **zeitgeistpublishing.com**